T0380832

Summer Chillers

WE MAKE CHILLING FUN FOR EVERYONE

K. MacDonald

AuthorHouse™
1663 Liberty Drive
Bloomington, IN 47403
www.authorhouse.com
Phone: 833-262-8899

Because of the dynamic nature of the Internet, any web addresses or links contained in this book may have changed since publication and may no longer be valid. The views expressed in this work are solely those of the author and do not necessarily reflect the views of the publisher, and the publisher hereby disclaims any responsibility for them.

This book is printed on acid-free paper.

ISBN: 978-1-6655-6917-0 (sc)
ISBN: 978-1-6655-6918-7 (e)

Library of Congress Control Number: 2022915822

Print information available on the last page.

Published by AuthorHouse 08/31/2022

authorHOUSE®

Dedication

This book is dedicated to family and friends who have inspired and encouraged me to write this book. I hope everyone enjoys using this book as much as I did write it.

Introduction

We filled Summer Chillers with wonderful refreshing recipes that everyone in the family will enjoy this summer. From unique flavored ice cream, popsicles, shakes, and refreshing smoothies to refreshing non-alcohol drinks, that the entire family will love for those summer BBQ's. We have added many wonderful summer alcohol drinks that everyone will rave about. May Summer Chiller cool refreshing recipes bring tradition and happy memories into your home.

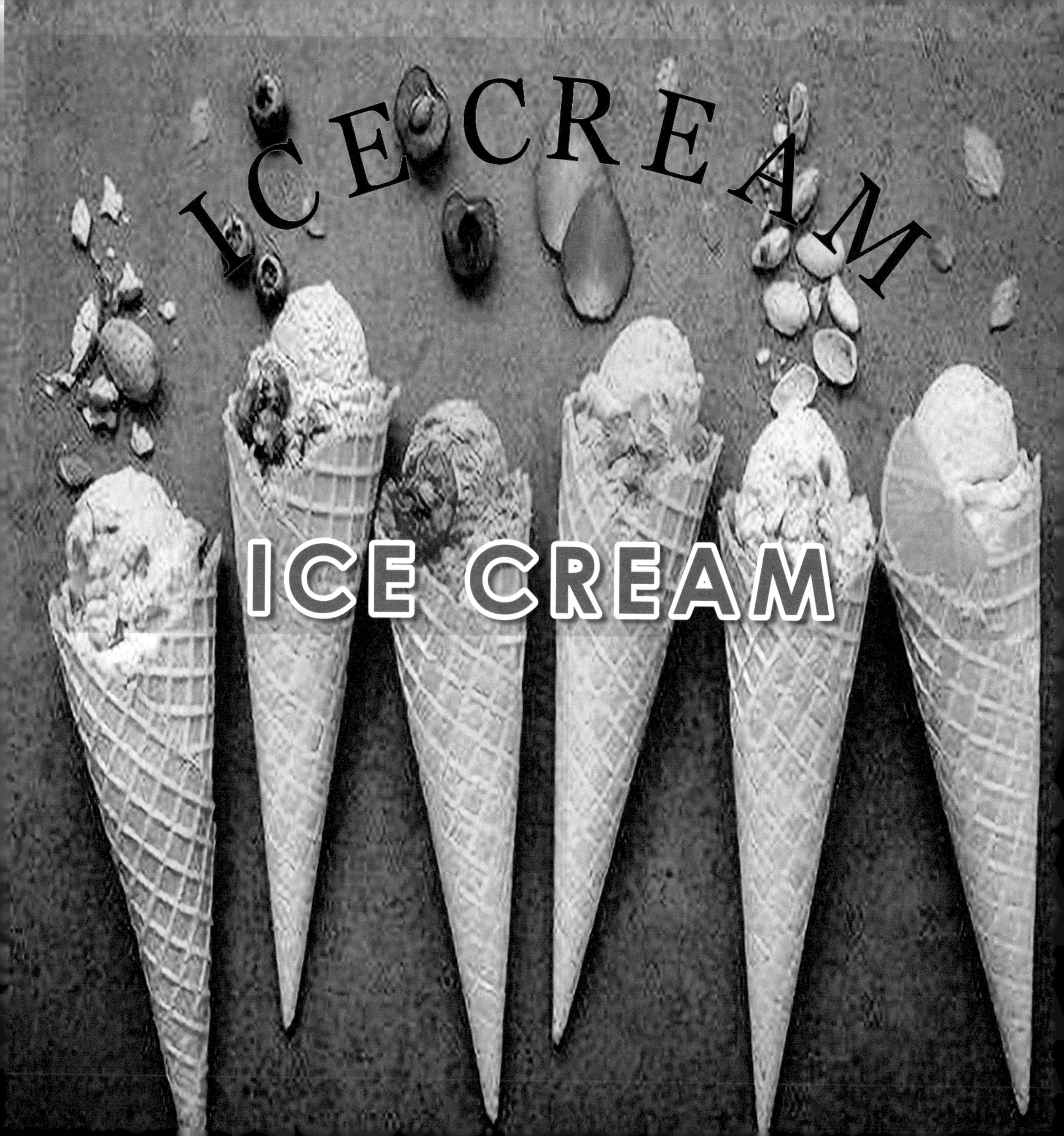
ICE CREAM
ICE CREAM

CONTENTS

Ice Cream Sandwiches

INGREDIENTS

½ cup butter

½ cup semi-sweet chocolate chips

1/3 cup sugar 1 egg

1 tsp. Vanilla ¾ cup flour

2 Tbsp. cocoa powder

½ tsp. baking powder

3 cups vanilla Ice cream

slightly softened

DIRECTIONS

Pre heat oven to 325 degrees. Line 10 x 15 cookie sheet with wax paper & lightly oil paper.

Melt butter and chocolate chips.

Stir and allow to cool. Beat together sugar and egg until creamy and pale. Beat in melted chocolate and vanilla. Add flour, cocoa powder, baking powder. Continue beating until incorporated.

Transfer batter to pan and spread evenly to edges. Bake 15 minutes, then remove from oven.

Cool 10 minutes and invert onto cutting board. Carefully remove wax paper and using a sharp un-serrated knife, cut in half lengthwise. When completely cool, spread ice-cream over one half of the chocolate biscuit evenly. Top with second wafer, wrap in plastic wrap and freeze for at least 4 hours. Cut into 8 slices.

Birthday Cake Ice Cream

INGREDIENTS:

1 cup milk

1 tsp. vanilla

½ cup sugar

2 cups heavy whipping cream

2 egg yolks, beaten

1 cup party cake mix

1 small jar favorite sprinkles

DIRECTIONS

Whisk together milk, sugar, egg yolks, vanilla, cream, and cake mix in a saucepan until well blended.

Cook over medium-low heat until mixture reaches 160 degrees F (70 degrees C), stirring often.

Remove from heat and let cool until warm then cover with plastic wrap making sure plastic wrap is touching the cream mixture. Let cool completely at room temperature about 1 hour. Then place in the refrigerator until liquid is cold for 1 hour.

Pour the chilled mixture into an ice cream maker and churn according to manufacturer's directions until it reaches a peak.

Transfer ice cream to a lidded plastic freezer container. Fold in your favorite birthday cake sprinkle toppings, Cover and freeze for 4-6 hour or for best results overnight.

Georgia Peach Ice Cream

INGREDIENTS

2 cups Ripe peaches freshly chopped

2 Large eggs

1 ¾ cup sugar

2 cup heavy or whipping cream

juice of 1 lemon

1 cup milk

1 cup peach juice or nectar

DIRECTIONS

Combine the peaches, ¾ cup of the sugar and the lemon juice in a bowl. Cover and refrigerate for 1 hours stirring every 15 minutes Remove peaches from the refrigerator and drain the juice into a small bowl. Return the peaches to the refrigerator.

In a medium saucepan on medium high heat stirring constantly combine remaining 1 cup sugar, Fresh peach juice, peach nectar, beaten eggs, heavy cream milk. Heat until sugar has dissolved Do not boil. Let cool completely before transferring mixture to ice cream container. Once cooled transfer the mixture to the ice cream maker and churn following manufacturer instructions. When ice cream can form a peak add the peaches then continue to churn ice cream for additional 2 minutes. Transfer ice cream to a lidded freezer container cover and freeze for 4-6 hour. For best result freeze overnight.

Pear Sorbet

INGREDIENTS

7 small pears, peeled and sliced

3/4 cup sugar

2/3 cup white grape juice

2/3 cup pear nectar

1 ½ Tbsp.lemon juice

DIRECTIONS

In a large saucepan, combine all ingredients. Bring to a boil. Reduce heat simmer uncovered for 8-10minutes or until pears are tender. Cool slightly. Pour in the blender or food processor, cover, and process for 1-2 minute or until smooth. Transfer lidded freezer container cover and freeze until firm. Just before serving, process again in food processor for 1-2 minutes or until smooth. Spoon sorbet into individual dessert dishes. Serve at once.

Cherry Chunk Ice Cream

INGREDIENTS

4 Hershey's chocolate bar chopped

¼ cup cherries halved & pitted

2 large eggs

¾ cup sugar

2 cups heavy cream

1 cup milk

DIRECTIONS

Place the shaved chocolate flakes and the cherries in separate bowls. Cover and refrigerate. Whisk the eggs in a mixing bowl, slowly whisk in sugar a little at a time. Whisk until completely blended.

Pour in the cream and milk and whisk until blended. Transfer the mixture to the ice cream maker and freeze following manufacturer's instructions. 2 minutes before it is done churning add the chocolate shavings and cherries continue to blend an additional 2 minutes. Transfer ice cream to a freezer safe lidded container, cover finish freezing in freezer until firm.

Blueberry Cheesecake Ice Cream

INGREDIENTS

8 oz. cream cheese

¼ cup sugar

1 tsp. vanilla

2 cups heavy cream

1 ½ cups blueberries

1 cup milk

1 cup sugar

4 squares graham crackers

1 tsp lemon juice

DIRECTIONS

Boil blueberries and sugar in small saucepan until berries and the mixture has thickened (7-8minutes). Cool completely set aside. In a mixing bowl combine heavy cream, milk, and vanilla, lemon juice, and zest. Set aside ½ cup blueberry sauce for dessert sauce if desired. Chill cream cheese mixture in refrigerator for several hours or until cold. Freeze ice cream in an ice cream maker according to directions, 2 minutes before ice cream is done churning add remaining blueberries, sauce, and the graham cracker crust pieces, mix for 2 additional minutes.

Transfer ice cream to a lidded freezer container, cover and freeze in freezer for 2-3 hours or until firm. Serve with reserved blueberry sauce.

Apple Pie Ice Cream

INGREDIENTS

1 -15oz can apple pie filling

¾ cup sugar

2 large eggs

2 cups heavy whipping cream

1 cup whole milk

3 graham crackers, chopped

DIRECTIONS

Using a sharp knife, cut the pie filling into ¼ inch chunks, set aside until last 2 minutes before ice cream is competed. Whisk the egg in a mixing bowl until light and fluffy 1-2 minutes then continue to whisk in sugar, vanilla until completely blended.

Transfer the mixture to ice cream maker and freeze following manufacturer's instructions. 2 minutes before ice cream can form a peak add the pie filling graham cracker pieces. Continue to churn for 2 minutes, then transfer ice cream to an airtight container and finish freezing in the freezer until firm.

Key Lime Pie Ice Cream

INGREDIENTS

½ cup sugar

1 egg yolk

2 Tbsp. cornstarch

1 tsp. key lime zest

1/8 tsp salt

1/3 cup key lime juice

2 cups milk

½ cup crushed graham crackers

1 cup half & half

DIRECTIONS

Whisk together the first 3 ingredients is a large heavy saucepan. Gradually whisk in milk

And half and half. Cook over medium heat. Stirring constantly, 8 to 10 minutes or until

Mixture thickens slightly.

Remove from heat. Whisk egg yolk until thickened. Gradually whisk about 1 cup hot cream mixture into yolk. Add yolk to remaining cream mixture, whisking constantly. Pour mixture through a fine wire mesh strainer into a bowl discard solid. Cooling 1 hour, stirring occasionally. Place plastic wrap directly on cream mixture, chill 8 to 24 hours. Pour mixture into ice cream maker and freeze according to manufacturer's instructions. Just before ice cream can peak add key lime juice, key lime zest and graham cracker pieces continue mixing in ice cream maker for additional 2-3 minutes or until ice cream has peaked. Transfer to airtight container and finish freezing in freezer until firm.

Strawberry Shortcake Ice Cream

INGREDIENTS:

12 oz sliced strawberries

1 cup sour cream

1 Tbsp. lemon juice

2 cup milk chocolate chopped

8oz. cream cheese

½ cup half and half

1 cup sugar pinch of salt

DIRETIONS

In a blender or food processor puree the strawberries, cream cheese, sour cream, half and half, lemon juice, salt. Transfer the mixture to ice cream maker and freeze following manufacturer's instructions. In a bowl mix together strawberries and remaining sugar and set aside. 2 minutes before done churning add the strawberries and chocolate chunks then continue freezing until the ice cream can form a peak. Transfer ice cream to an airtight container finish freezing in freezer until it is firm.

Chocolate Peanut Butter Ice Cream

INGREDIENTS:

Peanut Butter Filling

¾ cup sugar

2 ½ cups whole milk

¾ cup smooth peanut butter

1/3 cup unsweetened cocoa powder

¾ cup heavy cream Pinch of salt

3 Tbsp. cornstarch

1 cup milk

1 Tbsp +1 tsp heavy cream

DIRECTIONS

In a small bowl whisk together the sugar, cocoa powder, and cornstarch. In a heavy bottom saucepan, warm milk over medium heat. Add sugar mixture to the warm milk and whisk out any lumps. Continue to heat over medium heat until the mixture just starts to boil. It will be a thick consistency of chocolate pudding. Pour the chocolate mixture through a fine mesh strainer into a large bowl. Add the heavy cream and ¾ cup of the chocolate to the bowl. Stir the cream into the chocolate mixture until melts and is a smooth consistency. Put plastic wrap directly over the chocolate mixture- making sure it touches the mix. This keeps a thick skin from forming on your ice cream base. Refrigerate at least two hours, overnight if possible. While the chocolate base is cooling make your peanut butter swirl. You want to make the peanut butter swirl the same day you will be churning your ice cream. In a small bowl, whisk Together the peanut butter, heavy cream, and salt. Cover with plastic wrap and set aside at room temperature. When your chocolate mixture is completely cool, churn it according to manufacturer's instructions. When completely churned, add remaining ¼ cup chocolate into the mixture, stirring completely throughout the ice cream. Spoon into an airtight container. Add droppings of peanut butter on top of the ice cream. Swirl it in with a butter knife or stiff spatula. Mix peanut butter throughout ice cream but still chunky consistency. Cover and freeze in freezer until firm.

Velvety Smooth Chocolate Ice Cream

INGREDIENTS

¾ cup sugar

2 Tbsp. unsweetened cocoa powder

4 egg yolk, beaten

2 cups heavy cream

½ cup half and half 1 tsp vanilla

½ cup whole milk

2 oz. milk chocolate

¼ tsp salt

DIRECTIONS

In a saucepan combine the sugar, salt cocoa powder. Whisk thoroughly so that There are no lumps of cocoa powder. While whisking slowly add the milk, half and half. Turn the heat to medium low. Stir constantly and bring to a simmer. Just bubbles form on the side of the pan Remove from the heat and set aside. Place the egg yolks in a small bowl and beat well. Gradually stir ½ cup of the hot Liquid to the egg yolks slowly drizzle the egg yolks into the saucepan with the hot liquid stirring constantly. Place saucepan over low heat until thickened and coats back of s spoon. Do not boil mixture. Remove from heat stir in chopped chocolate until completely melted. Pour mixture through a fine mesh strainer into a bowl. Place chocolate mixture on top of an ice bath. Stir every 2 minutes for 10 minutes then place in refrigerator for 2 hours. Once chilled pour into ice cream maker and churn until stiff. Transfer to airtight container finish freezing in freezer until firm.

Deep Fried Ice Cream

INGREDIENTS

20 oz. favorite ice cream

2 cups 4 grain cereal, crushed

1 ½ Tbsp. sugar

3 ½ tsp. ground cinnamon

2 eggs

1 tsp. water

4 (8-inch) flour tortilla

Oil for frying

Whipped cream

maraschino cherries

DIRECTIONS

Form ice cream into 4 balls. Place in baking pan and freeze solid, 2 hours or longer. Mix cereal sugar and cinnamon. Divide equally between 2 pie plates or other shallow containers. Beat eggs with water. Roll each ice cream ball into cereal mixture and press coating into ice cream. Dip coated ball into egg wash, then roll in container of cereal a second time. Again, press coating into ice cream Freeze coated ice cream balls solid 4 to 6 hours. Shape each tortilla into hourglass form (with narrow waist) by cutting off curved slices from 2 opposite sides. One end will serve as base for ice cream. Another end will be a decorative fan. Heat oil in wok or large deep fryer. Place tortilla between ladles or large spoons of varied sizes. Smaller ladle on top. Place tortilla so that base end is cupped in larger ladle to form a basket with back of upper fan supported by handle of larger ladle. Deep fry until crisp, Drain and sprinkle with cinnamon sugar. Set aside Deep fry frozen coated ice cream ball for 30-45 seconds. Place each fried tortilla in a large, stemmed glass or bowl with fan tortilla. Top with dollop of whipped cream and a decorative cherry.

Silky Smooth Vanilla Ice Cream

INGREDIENTS

1 1/3 cup sugar

¼ tsp salt

3 cups heavy cream

8 egg yolks

1 cup whole milk

1 Tbsp. vanilla extract

DIRECTIONS

Pour the cream/egg mixture back into the pan and heat over medium low stirring constantly until thickens and coats the back of a spoon. A few bubbles may come up along edges but never boil. Remove from the heat add the vanilla. Set a fine mesh strainer over a large bowl.

Pour the warm ice cream mixture through the strainer into the bowl. Cool the mixture over an ice bath stirring every few minutes. After 10-15 minutes place the mixture in the refrigerator until completely chilled. Set up your ice cream machine according to directions. With the machine running add the mixture in a slow steady stream, churn until stiffens. Transfer into an airtight container finish freezing in freezer until firm. freezer for several hours to firm up. Serve with your choice of toppings!

Berry White Popsicle

INGREDIENTS

1¾ cup whole milk

1 Tbsp. honey

¼ tsp. vanilla

1 (12oz. pkg. frozen or fresh berries

Divided

DIRECTIONS

Whisk together in a small bowl, whole milk, honey, vanilla. Evenly divide and drain mixed berries into popsicle molds. Once berries are divided pour milk mixture over berries.

Huckleberry Cheesecake Popsicle

CRUST

4 Tbsp. crushed graham crackers

INGREDIENTS

1 cup huckleberries

½ cup water

½ cup water

1 ½ Tbsp agave

¼ cup cream cheese

½ cup milk

1 Tbsp agave nectar

DIRECTIONS

Add huckleberries, water and agave nectar to a blender and puree for 45 seconds. Pour into a measuring cup and set aside. Rinse the blender. Add cream cheese, milk, agave, puree for 45 seconds or until all the lumps are gone. Top with mold holders or insert sticks. Freeze 4-6 hours or until solid

Lemon Cream Popsicles

INGREDIENTS:

1 (14oz. can) sweetened condensed milk

1 cup whole milk

½ cup fresh lemon juice

1/3 cup sugar

½. grated lemon

DIRECTIONS

In a bowl whisk together all ingredients until sugar is dissolved.

Pour into molds top with holders or insert sticks.

Freeze for 6-8 hours or until solid.54

Almond Fudge Popsicles

INGREDIENTS

2 cups whole milk

1-3.9 oz. pkg. chocolate fudge
Instant pudding

1/8 tsp almond extract

½ cup sugar

½ cup amaretto nondairy creamer

DIRECTIONS

In a bowl whisk together all ingredients for 2 minutes or until creamy.

Pour Into popsicle molds or small cups. Top with molds holders or stick.

Freeze for 4-6 hours or until solid.

Oreo Popsicles

INGREDIENTS

1 ½ cups vanilla yogurt

¼ cup whole milk

¼ cup cream cheese

15 crushed Oreo's

DIRECTIONS

In a medium bowl whisk together the yogurt, cream cheese, sugar, and vanilla.

Once smooth stir in the crushed cookies.

Pour into the popsicle molds leaving a little space at the top for them to expand. Tap firmly on the counter to remove any bubbles.

Insert the mold holders and freeze until firm at least 4 fours.

Remove from freezer and run the mold under warm water for a few seconds to loosen the popsicles from the molds then gently pull on the popsicle stick to remove the mold completely. enjoy

SHAKES & SMOOTHIES

CONTENTS

Honey Almond Peach

INGREDIENTS

1½ tsp. Almond syrup

1 medium ripe banana, frozen

1cup (8oz.) vanilla yogurt

2cups fresh sliced small peaches

1 Tbsp. lemon juice

1 Tbsp. Honey

1 tsp. grated lemon peel

6 ice cubes

DIRECTIONS

In a blender or food processor combine all the ingredients. Cover and Process until smooth. Pour into glasses. Serve at once.

Banana Crush

DIRECTIONS

cups sugar

6cup water

5 crushed bananas

1 small can frozen orange juice

1 lg can pineapple juice

Juice of 2 lemons

1 liter 7 up

DIRECTIONS

Combine sugar, water, heat until sugar has completely dissolved. Allow to cool.

Add the fruit and juice and freeze 4-6 hours or until solid. When ready to serve add

1/2 cup of the frozen mixture in a glass and fill with 7-Up.

Strawberry Smoothie

INGREDIENTS

2 cups strawberries

5 ice cubes

1-8oz. carton vanilla yogurt

1 Tbsp orange juice

2 tsp. sugar

2 tsp brown sugar

1 ½ tsp. honey

1 tsp lemon juice

Whipped topping

DIRECTIONS

In a blender, combine the first 8 ingredients. Cover and process

Until smooth. Pour into chilled glasses. Garnish with whipped topping if desired.

Serve at once.

Blackberry Smoothie

INGREDIENTS

1cup orange juice

1cup plain yogurt

2 Tbsp. honey

½cup mixed berries

DIRECTIONS

In a blender, combine all ingredients, cover, and process until smooth.

Pour into a chilled glass, serve at once.

Cherry Berry Smoothie

INGREDIENTS

½cup frozen cherries

½ cup frozen raspberries

1cup coconut milk

½ cups frozen raspberries

ice

DIRECTIONS

Add all ingredients to blender. Blend until mixture becomes smooth & thick. Pour into favorite glass and enjoy.

Layered Fruit Smoothie

INGREDIENTS

1 Mango peeled & Chopped

1 ¼ cups plain yogurt

4 Tbsp. honey

1 Tbsp. fresh lime juice

¼ tsp. grated lime zest

1 banana peeled, chopped

10 medium strawberries

¼ tsp. grated lemon zest

DIRECTIONS

In a blender, blend the mango, ¾ yogurt and 2 Tbsp. honey the fresh lime juice; 2 ice cubes and the freshly grated lime zest until smooth. Divide mango lime smoothie between 2 straight sided glassed and set aside. Rinse blender then blend the banana, strawberries ½ cup yogurt, 2 Tbsp honey, fresh lemon juice 2 ice cubes. banana, strawberry smoothie onto mango smoothie, gently spooning mixture down inside edge of each glass to create horizontal line.

Pb & J Smoothie

INGREDIENTS

2 ½ cups milk

3 bananas, frozen sliced

3 Tbsp. peanut butter with honey

3 Tbsp. fruit spread

DIRECTIONS

Pour the milk into a blender cut the bananas into slices and add them to the milk. Add the peanut butter and Fruit spread. Blend until Smooth.

Raspberry Mango Smoothie

INGREDIENTS

1 cup raspberries

2 cups ice

1 ¾ cup orange juice

1 cup mango

1 Tbsp. honey juice of 1 lemon

½ tsp. turmeric

2 Tbsp. water

2 tsp. freshly grated ginger

DIRECTIONS

Make the first layer by combining raspberries, orange juice, honey, turmeric, In a blender. Add ice and process until smooth. Add more juice and water to thin it out or add more ice to thicken it.

Mango layer

Blend mango, orange juice, lemon, water, ginger and ice and process until smooth. Slowly pour mango layer over the berry layer and serve.

Green Tea Kiwi & Mango Smoothie

INGREDIENTS

2 ½ cups frozen diced mango

¾ cup vanilla yogurt, divided

¼ cup honey divided

2 Tbsp. water

½ tsp. lime zest

3 kiwi fruits, peeled, quartered

2 cups ice cubes

½ cup packed baby spinach

2 Tbsp. bottled green tea

DIRECTIONS

Place mango, ½ cup yogurt 2 Tbsp honey 2 Tbsp water and lime zest in a blende process until smooth, stirring occasionally. Divide mango mixture into 4 serving glasses. Place glasses in freezer. Rinse blender container place ¼ cup yogurt, 2 Tbsp. honey kiwi fruit, ice cubes, ½ cup packed baby spinach, 2 Tbsp. bottled green tea in blender. Process in a blender until smooth, stirring occasionally. Gently spoon green tea- kiwi mixture onto mango mixture in reserved glasses, working carefully around inside of glass to create a clean horizontal line. Garnish with kiwi fruit slices and stir to combine flavors if desired.

Serve at once.

Coconut Milk Smoothie

INGREDIENTS

3 Bananas

½ cup yogurt

3 Tbsp. honey

1 cup coconut milk

10oz. frozen berries or

fruit your choice

DIRECTIONS

Put coconut milk banana, honey yogurt berries or fruit into blender.

Blend it until it becomes smooth Serve at once.

Mango Smoothie

INGREDIENTS

1 ½ cups mango nectar

1 banana cut in half

¾ cup vanilla yogurt

1 ½ cup frozen mango chunks

Lime slices and mint

sprigs for garnish

DIRECTIONS

Place the mango nectar banana yogurt, mango chunks in the blender.

Blend until completely smooth.

Pour into 2 glasses and serve, garnished with lime

And mint if desired.

Pineapple Banana Shake

INGREDIENTS

1 can (8 oz.) crushed pineapple, undrained

1 cup buttermilk

1 Tbsp. Honey

1/8 tsp coconut extract

DIRECTIONS

In a food processor or blender, combine all ingredients cover and blend until smooth.

Pour into glasses. Serve at once.

Frappuccino

INGREDIENTS

½ cup fresh expresso

¼ cup sugar

2 ½ cup (2% milk)

1 Tbsp. dry pectin

DIRECTION

Combine all ingredients in a blender. Blend for 30 seconds until

Sugar and pectin are dissolved

Banana Shake

INGREDIENTS

1 cup half & half cream

4 cups vanilla ice cream, softened

1 medium banana sliced

¼ tsp. banana extract

DIRECTIONS

In a blender combine all ingredients cover and blend until smooth.

Pour into a chilled glass and enjoy.

Mixed Berry

INGREDIENTS

1 quart vanilla ice cream

6oz strawberries

6oz blueberries

6oz blackberries

2 cups whole milk

DIRECTIONS

In a blender combine all ingredients except ice cream. Blend until smooth.

Blend in ice cream until berry mixture is incorporated and mixture is thick.

Serve at once.

Dreamsicle

INGREDIENTS

8scoops vanilla ice cream softened

4cups orange soda, chilled

¼ tsp orange extract

Whipped cream

DIRECTIONS

Place 2 scoops ice cream in each 16 oz. glass.

In a large pitcher combine the soda and extract, Pour soda over ice cream and top with whipped cream is desired. Serve at once.

Old Fashioned Soda

INGREDIENTS

¾ cup chocolate syrup

4cups carbonated water

1cup whole milk

8scoops ice cream

Whipped cream

Maraschino cherry

DIRECTIONS

Place 3 Tbsp syrup in each 16 oz. glass.

Add ¼ cup milk and 1 cup carbonated water to each glass.

Stir until foamy. Add 2 scoops ice cream to each glass and top with whipped cream

and a maraschino cherry

NON-ALCOHOLIC BEVERAGE

CONTENTS

Watermelon Lime Slushy

INGREDIENTS

Chunked seedless watermelon

Lime juice

Ice

Lime wedges for garnish

DIRECTIONS

Add all ingredients to blender and process until the ice gets totally crushed and has no lumps of watermelon. The amount of lime juice used depends on how tangy You want the slushy to be. You can also add sweetener if you want the slushy to be sweeter. Pour in favorite glass and enjoy.

Sensational Slushy

INGREDIENTS

½ cup sugar

1 pkg. strawberry gelatin

2 cups boiling water

2 cups fresh strawberries, sliced

1 cup pineapple juice

1 can frozen lemonade

1 can frozen limeade

2 cup ice water

2 liters 7-up, chilled

DIRECTIONS

In a large bowl, dissolve sugar and gelatin in boiling water. Place the strawberries and pineapple juice in a blender or food processor cover, and process until smooth. Add gelatin mixture. Stir in frozen lemonade limeade, and chilled. Cover and freeze for 8 hours or overnight. Remove from the freezer 45 minutes before serving. For each serving combine ½ cup slush mixture with ½ cup 7-up stir well. Serve at once.

Strawberry Slushy

INGREDIENTS

1 pkg. frozen sweetened sliced strawberries, thawed

2 liters 7 up soda, chilled

1 can (12 oz.) frozen pink lemonade concentrate, thawed

DIRECTIONS

Place the strawberries in a blender, cover a process until pureed.

Pour into a pitcher. Stir in the soda and lemonade concentrate.

Serve immediately

Lavender Lemonade

INGREDIENTS:

Lemonade Coconut water

Lavender simple syrup Dried lavender sprigs

Sugar Water

Violet food coloring Lemon slices for garnish

Mint for garnish

DIRECTIONS:

Combine lemonade, coconut water, and water in a tall glass. Add lavender simple syrup to the mixture, again stir and serve. You can garnish your drink with a lemon slice or lavender. The amount of lavender simple syrup depends on your taste.

Lavender Simple Syrup

Take a saucepan and combine about 2 Tbsp. dried lavender, 2 cups sugar, 1 ½ cups of water. On high heat, boil it for 1 minute. Remove heat and cover it for about 25 minutes. Then using a fine mesh sieve, strain the lavender from the syrup and let the syrup cool. Then add few drops of violet food coloring to the syrup and your lavender simple syrup is ready.

Fresh Lemonade

INGREDIENTS

Lemonade

1 cup freshly squeezed lemon juice

Coconut water

½ to ¾ cup superfine sugar, to taste

Lavender simple syrup

1 cup crushed ice

Dried lavender sprigs

4 cups water

Sugar water

Violet food coloring

Lemon slices for garnish

Mint for garnish

DIRECTIONS

Place all ingredients in a blender and process until completely smooth.

Serve over ice.

Minty Lemonade

INGREDIENTS

Lemon juice Lemon wheel for garnish

Mint leaves Ice cubes

Honey

DIRECTIONS

Put lemon juice, mint leaves, ice cubes, in the pitcher. Add water to the mixture. Put in honey then stir. Garnish with lemon wheels and mint leaves. All flavors are measured by your desired taste

Blueberry Lemonade

INGREDIENTS

1 ¼ cups sugar

1 cup blueberries

2 2/3 boiling water

2 cups lemon juice

7 cups chilly water

DIRECTIONS:

Muddle 1 ¼ cups sugar and 1 cup blueberries in a bowl with a muddler or wooden spoon until berries are well mashed. Add 2 2/3 cups boiling water let stand until steam stops rising from bowl, about 10 minutes. Strain through a wire mesh strainer into a 3-quart pitcher or drink dispenser, discarding solids. Stir in 2 cups freshly squeezed lemon juice (about 10 lemons) and 7 cup chilly water. Chill until cold, at least 1 hour. Serve over Ice.

Raspberry Lemonade Spritzer

INGREDIENTS:

Lemonade concentrate

Sparkling water

1 Tbsp. of raspberry jam

Juice of ½ lemon

Fresh raspberries

DIRECTIONS

Squash 4 raspberries in a glass, stir in 1 Tbsp of raspberry

Jam. Add some of the lemonade and stir to combine. Fill glass with ice.

Top with sparkling water and fresh lemon juice.

Decorate with raspberries and slice of lemon.

Sunshine Spritzer

INGREDIENTS

½ gallon orange juice

2 small cans pineapple juice

1 Tbsp lemon juice

1 small pkg. frozen sliced strawberries

2 cans 7 up Ice

DIRECTIONS

In a pitcher mix orange juice, lemon juice, pineapple juice. Add sliced strawberries. Mix juice and Berries together. Add 2 cans of 7 up mix well. Pour over ice and serve.

Raspberry Mint Cooler

INGREDIENTS:

2 cups water

1 ½ cups chopped mint

¾ cup sugar

3 pkg.10 oz. each frozen raspberry

2 ¼ lemonade concentrate

6 cups chilly water

Crushed ice

DIRECTIONS:

In a large saucepan, bring the water, mint, and sugar to a boil.

Stir until sugar is dissolved. Remove from the heat; let stand for 5 minutes.

Add the raspberries and the lemonade concentrate, gently mash raspberries.

Line a strainer with four layers of cheesecloth; place over a 1-gallon container.

Slowly pour raspberry mixture into strainer, discard pulp and mint.

Add chilled water to the raspberry and stir well.

Serve in chilled glasses over crushed ice.

Cranberry Kiss

INGREDIENTS:

3 cups ginger ale

5 cups cranberry juice

1 ½ cups orange juice

Ice cubes

Fresh cranberries for decoration

DIRECTIONS:

Combine the cranberry juice

With orange juice in a pitcher. Add ginger ale and give it a good stir.

Add ice cubes tip it with fresh cranberries and serve.

Mango Mule

INGREDIENTS

Mango puree`

Ginger ale

Freshly squeezed lime juice

Mango slices or lime wedges

Ice cubes

DIRECTIONS

Put mango puree, ginger ale, lime juice, and ice cubes in a pitcher.

Stir well and transfer into the serving glass. Garnish it with a mango slice or lime wheel and enjoy an icy drink.

Sweet Tea

INGREDIENTS:

For the Simple Syrup

1 cup water

1 cup sugar

For the Iced Tea

7 cups water

2-3 family-size cold brew tea bags

DIRECTIONS

Put mango puree, ginger ale, lime juice, ice cubes in a pitcher.

Stir well. Pour into serving glass.

Garnish with mango and lime slices and enjoy and icy drink

Lemon Iced Tea

INGREDIENTS

1 ½ cups sugar

5 1/3 cups brewed black tea

1 ½ cups lemon juice

Lemon slices for garnish

DIRECTIONS:

Stir the sugar into the tea until dissolved. Add the lemon juice and stir until fully combined.

Chill completely in the refrigerator and serve over ice.

Garnished with lemon slices if desired

Cold Brewed Coffee

INGREDIENTS:

Cold brewed coffee

Sweetened Condensed milk

Ice cubes

DIRECTIONS:

Take a tall jar and fill it with ice cubes. Pour the cold- brewed coffee

in the glass and add the sweetened condensed milk. Stir it well and enjoy

chilled ice coffee

Cold brewed Coffee: to brew coffee you will need coffee and water. Put coffee in a glass or jar, add water to it and stir well. Cover the glass or jar and leave it for a night use a paper coffee filter or fine sieve to strain the coffee from the mixture. In this cold brew coffee is prepared. This coffee can be refrigerated for about 24 hours.

Frappuccino

INGREDIENTS

½ cup fresh expresso

¼ cup sugar

2 ½ cup (2% milk)

1 Tbsp. dry pectin

DIRECTION

Combine all ingredients in a blender. Blend for 30 seconds until sugar and pectin are dissolved

Arnold Palmer

INGREDIENTS

Mint leaves

½ cup fresh lemonade ½ cup unsweetened iced tea

Ice Sugar to your taste

Lemon for garnish Mint for garnish

DIRECTIONS

Take a few mint leaves in a tall glass and using a spoon crush the mint . between the glass and the spoon until you get the oil coming oil coming out of the leaves. Then add lots of ice to the glass. Add lemonade and unsweetened iced tea into the glass and give it a good stir. Top the drink with lemon wedges, mint sprigs, or both. If you want to make it sweeter you can add sugar to the lemonade or use sweet tea.

7-Up Punch

INGREDIENTS

1 lg. can frozen orange juice

4 cups sugar

1 can frozen lemonade

1 can frozen fruit juice

10 cups water

1 liter 7- up soda

DIRECTIONS

In a large pan combine the first 4 ingredients and 2 cup water, bring to a boil.

Once brought to a boil remove from heat. Add 8 cups water mix well.

Pour into quart jugs and freeze. Add one quart mix with 1 liter of 7 up and mix well.

Pour into glass of choice

Hawaiian Punch

INGREDIENTS

1 lg. can frozen orange juice

4 cups sugar

10 cups water

1 can frozen lemonade

1 lg. frozen fruit juice

1 liter 7- Up soda

DIRECTIONS

In a large pitcher or bowl combine orange juice, sugar, water, lemonade and

fruit juice. Stir until all ingredients are dissolved. Refrigerate.

Right before serving add 7-Up to the mixture, give a quick stir and serve over ice.

Shirley Temple

INGREDIENTS

½ cup orange juice

½ cup 7-Up

1 Tbsp grenadine syrup

1 maraschino cherry

DIRECTIONS

In a tall glass, combine orange juice and 7-Up.

Add grenadine and let it sink to the bottom.

Garnish with a maraschino cherry and whipped cream

Raspberry Vanilla Cream Soda

INGREDIENTS

2 Tbsp.Red Raspberry syrup

½ Tbsp. Vanilla syrup

1 cup sparkling water

1/4 cup. cold milk or half & half

ice

DIRECTIONS

Pour sparking water into tall glass filled with ice.

Add Syrup and stir well. Slowly top with milk

COLD ALCOHOLIC BEVERAGES

CONTENTS

Peachy Keen Daquiri

INGREDIENTS

2 ½ cups ice cubes

3 medium peaches peeled, sliced

¾ thawed, frozen limeade

¼ cup orange juice

2 Tbsp powdered sugar

½ cup rum

Grenadine syrup

DIRECTIONS

In a blender combine the ice, peaches, limeade concentrate, orange juice powdered sugar and rum if desired cover and process for 30 seconds or until smooth. Pour into a chilled glass. Add grenadine syrup, if desired. Serve at once.

Long Island Iced Tea

INGREDIENTS

1 oz. vodka

1 oz. gin

1 oz. white rum

½ oz triple sec

¼ Tbsp limeade

½ cup cola

2 lemon wedges

DIRECTIONS

Place vodka, gin, white rum, triple sec, and limeade in a cocktail shaker filled with ice.

Shake vigorously and then pour into highball glasses. Add dark cola or choice until the drink takes on iced tea color and stir gently. Garnish with lemon slices and serve.

Strawberry Mojito

INGREDIENTS

5 Limes

1 bunch

½ oz mint

1 cup white rum

½ cups strawberry syrup

2 cups chilled club soda

6 cups ice cubes

Sugar for rimming the glasses

6 strawberries for garnish

DIRECTIONS

Juice 4 limes and cut remaining lime into 6 wedges. Grasp mint sprig stems and leave against a work surface to help release the oil, transfer to sturdy glass pitcher Stir in, lime juice, rum, and strawberry syrup. Add club soda. Serve over ice in old fashioned cocktail glasses. Spread ¼ inch of sugar on a small shallow plate. Run a lime wedge around the rim of each glass. Then dip glass into sugar. Garnish with mint sprig and strawberries

Mojito

INGREDIENTS

1.5 OZ. Vodka

6-10 mint leaves

2 tsp sugar

2 tsp lime juice

1.5 oz soda water

DIRECTIONS

Gently crush mint leaves between your fingers and add to a cocktail shaker.

Fill the shaker with ice, vodka, simple syrup, and fresh lime juice.

Shake well and pour everything including the ice into a glass.

Top with soda water. Garnish with mint sprig and lime wedge.

Peachy Rye Julep

INGREDIENTS

2 Slices fresh peaches plus more for garnish

4 sprigs fresh mint plus more for garnish

2 tsp. turbinado sugar

1 ½ oz. rye whisky

2 dashes angostura bitters

1 ½ cup crushed ice

DIRECTIONS

In a silver julep or old fashion glass, muddle sliced fresh peaches, sprigs of fresh mint and turbinado sugar until peach is well Smashed and sugar is dissolved. Add rye whisky. Agnostus bitters and 1 cup crushed ice. Garnish with additional mint and peach slices. smashed and sugar is dissolved. Add rye whisky. Agnostus bitters and 1 cup crushed ice. Garnish with additional

Basil Cucumber Smash

INGREDIENTS

3 slices cucumber plus more for garnish

3 basil leaves plus mor for garnish

1 ½ tsp superfine sugar

1 ½ oz. vodka

1 cup ice

DIRECTIONS

In a Collins glass, muddle 3 slices cucumber 3 basil leaves and 1 ½ tsp superfine sugar until dissolved. Add 1 ½ oz vodka and 1 cup crushed ice. Stir until well chilled. Garnish with an additional cucumber slice and basil leaf.

Blackberry Rum Cobbler

INGREDIENTS

6 blackberries plus more for garnish

1 ½ tsp honey

1 ½ oz spiced rum

1 ½ cup crushed ice

DIRECTIONS

In a cocktail shaker muddle blackberries, honey, and crushed ice.

Shake until well chilled. Pour contents into an old-fashioned glass.

Mound ½ cup more crushed ice. Garnish with additional blackberries

And serve with straw.

Earlgrey Hound

INGREDIENTS

5 tsp. zest of grapefruit

¾ cup grapefruit sections

1 cup sugar

1 cup white wine vinegar

1 earl grey tea bag

1.5 oz vodka

DIRECTIONS

Earl Greyhound Starter: Zest grapefruit the section fruit, cutting it away from the peel and inner membrane. You should have 5 tsp zest and ¾ cup grapefruit sections. Pure` zest sections and any juices with sugar and white wine vinegar. Add earl grey tea bag chilled, cover 4 hours to 2 days. Remove tea bag and strain. Shrub keeps up to 3 weeks chilled. In a cocktail Shaker half filled with ice, combine 2 oz. earl grey starter and 1 ½ oz. vodka. Shake until very cold. Strain into martini glass or an ice filled old fashioned glass. Garnish with grapefruit

Blueberry Shrub

INGREDIENTS:

1 cup blueberries

1 cup sugar

1 cup red wine vinegar

½ tsp black peppercorn

½ oz. bourbon

3 oz ginger beer

Garnish Blueberries, Lime wedges

DIRECTIONS:

Blueberry Shrub Starter:

Puree blueberries, sugar, red wine vinegar in a blender. Add whole peppercorns and chill covered for 4 hours to 2 days. Strain into a mason jar. Starter keep up to 3 weeks chilled.

Blueberry Shrub:

In a cocktail shaker half filled with ice, combine 2 oz. stater and 1 ½ oz. bourbon. Shake until very cold strain into an ice filled pint glass. Top with 3 ounces ginger beer. Garnish with additional blueberries or lime wedge.

Cantaloupe Daquiri Shrub

INGREDIENTS

1 cubed cantaloupe

1 tsp. lime zest

1 cup sugar

1.5 oz. white rum

1 cup champagne vinegar

¾ oz. fresh lime juice

Garnish with sliced cantaloupe, limes

DIRECTIONS

Cantaloupe daiquiri Shrub Starter. Puree cubed cantaloupe Sugar, champagne, vinegar in a blender. Stir in 1 tsp lime zest. Chill cover for 4 hours up to 2 days. Strain shrub keeps up to 3 weeks chilled in a cocktail shaker half-filled with ice, combine 2 oz. cantaloupe shrub starter: white rum, lime juice. Shake until very cold. Strain into an ice filled wine glass or water goblet. Garnish with slices of cantaloupe and lime.

Spicy Watermelon Margarita

INGREDIENTS

2 cups cubed seedless watermelon

1 ½ oz silver tequila

¾ oz. Cointreau

¾ oz. lime juice

1 slice jalapeno

DIRECTIONS

Puree seedless watermelon in a blender. Wipe the rim of a margarita glass with a lime wedge. Dip rim into kosher salt or coarse white decorating sugar. In a cocktail shaker half filled with ice, add 2 oz. of the watermelon puree the silver tequila, Cointreau, lime juice, and jalapeno. Shake until very cold. Strain I not prepared glass. Float a jalapeno slice on top of drink.

Raspberry Mimosa

INGREDIENTS:

2 cups raspberries

¼ cup sugar to taste

Mint for garnish

1 bottle of champagne

Raspberries for garnish

DIRECTIONS

In a small saucepan, heat raspberries with sugar over medium heat until they have broken down and sugar has completely dissolved. Remove from heat and puree in blender or small food processor. Press the mixture through Sieve and set aside to cool down. When ready to serve add a dash of raspberry syrup to each champagne glass. Pour champagne with garnish each with raspberries and mint. You can also drop a few raspberries directly into your mimosa.

Clover Club

INGREDIENTS

5 fresh raspberries

¾ oz. simple syrup

1 sprig fresh thyme

¾ oz. lemon juice

1 ½ oz. gin

1 egg whites

Simple Syrup

1 cup water

1 cup sugar

Simple syrup:

In a mason jar sugar and water tightly close lid and shake until water has dissolved.

Clover Club:

In a cocktail shaker muddle raspberries and 1 sprig fresh thyme. Add gin, egg white simple syrup, fresh lemon juice. Shake until mixture no longer sounds sloshy. Add ice to shaker half full. Shake again until very cold. Strain into a cocktail glass. Dust top with cinnamon or garnish with lemon zest or additional thyme.

Red Snapper

INGREDIENTS:

2 pinches celery salt

2 pinches ground black pepper

1 lime wedges

2 oz. gin

4 oz. tomato juice

½ oz. lemon juice

6 dashes tabasco

4 dashes Worcestershire

DIRECTIONS

Pour the salt and pepper onto a small plate. Rub the juicy side of a lime wedge along the lip of a pint glass. Rim the glass with the salt and pepper And fill the glass ice. Add the remaining ingredients into a shaker with ice and shake until chilled. Strain into a prepared glass and garnish with celery stalk and lime wedge.

Sparkling Rose Margarita

INGREDIENTS

10 oz. Strawberry-basil infused Blanco tequila

5 oz. fresh lime juice

4 oz. agave syrup

1 bottle sparkling rose` (750ml)

Sliced strawberries for garnish

Lime wheel for garnish

DIRECTIONS

In a punch bowl, combine the tequila, lime juice and agave syrup.

Add cubed ice and stir with a ladle to mix. Top with the sparking rose`.

Garnish with 1 cup sliced strawberries and lime wheels from 2 limes.

Rim punch glasses with rose salt before serving. Strawberry basil infused Blanco tequila.

In a glass jar, combine ½ cup sliced strawberries and ½ cup fresh basil leaves with

1-750ml bottle Blanco tequila. Seal jar tightly and let sit unrefrigerated for 3-5 days.

Shake daily Strain out solids and rebottle the infused tequila Rose salt:

Add 4 Tbsp Sea salt and 1 Tbsp dried rose buds to a mortar and pestle, and gently grind.

Place on a small plate for rimming.

Pina Colada

INGREDIENTS:

2 oz. light rum

Garnish

1 ½ oz cream of coconut

Pineapple wedges

1 ½ oz. pineapple juice

Pineapple Leaf

½ oz. fresh lime juice

DIRECTIONS

Add the ingredients into a shaker with ice and shake vigorously 20-30 seconds.

Strain into a chilled hurricane glass over pebble ice. Garnish with a pineapple wedge and pineapple leaf.

Sparkling Watermelon Punch

INGREDIENTS

1 mini watermelon

6 mint leaves

4 oz. vodka

2 oz. fresh lime juice

1 oz. simple syrup

Sparkling wine to top

DIRECTIONS

With 1 large spoon or ice cream scoop, carve out the insides of half a mini watermelon and set aside. Add the watermelon chunks and mint leaves to a blender, and puree` until smooth. Fine strain the puree` to remove pulp and add the juice (about 1cup) to a separate container. In the carved watermelon half, add cubed ice, vodka, lime juice simple syrup, and 5 oz. watermelon juice. Top with the sparkling wine. Garnish with lime wheels and a mint sprig.

Strawberry Daquiri

INGREDIENTS

4 oz. aged Puerto Rican or Jamaican Rum

2 oz. Fresh lime juice

1 oz. Rich simple syrup (2 parts sugar 1 part water)

10 oz. strawberries

6 ice cubes

Garnish

Lime slices,
strawberry slices

DIRECTIONS

Add all ingredients into a blender a blend until smooth.

Pour into a margarita glass or wine goblet.

Garnish with lime slices or strawberry slices

Frozen Margarita

INGREDIENTS

2 oz. Blanco tequila

1 oz. Fresh lime juice

¾ oz. orange liqueur

Garnish

Salt rim, Lime wheel

DIRECTIONS

Salt the rim of a chilled margarita glass and put aside. Add all the ingredients into a blender. Top of with 1 cup of ice. Blend until the mixture is smooth and frothy. Pour the contents into a salted margarita glass. Garnish with a lime wheel.

Aviation Cocktail

INGREDIENTS

2 oz. maraschino liqueur

¼ oz Crème de Violette or crème Yvette

Garnish:

Brandied cherry

DIRECTIONS

Add ingredients into a shaker with ice and shake.

Strain into a cocktail glass. Garnish with a brandied cherry.

Dark & Stormy Cocktail

INGREDIENTS

1 ½ oz. Black seal rum

Stormy ginger beer, to top

Garnish

Lime wedge

DIRECTION

Fill a tall glass with ice and add the rum. Top with ginger beer.

Garnish with a lime wedge

The author was encouraged and inspired to write this book as a family cookbook. Through the process, has blossomed into more than she ever imagined.

Special thanks to all that shared their recipes making this book possible.

Printed in the United States
by Baker & Taylor Publisher Services